CW01213052

Original title:
From Shadows

Copyright © 2024 Swan Charm
All rights reserved.

Author: Liina Liblikas
ISBN HARDBACK: 978-9916-89-640-2
ISBN PAPERBACK: 978-9916-89-641-9
ISBN EBOOK: 978-9916-89-642-6

## Shrouded Whispers

In twilight's shade, secrets creep,
Through the woods, silence deep.
Leaves rustle soft, in muted flight,
Echoes linger, in the night.

A lantern's glow, flickers dim,
Guides the lost, on a whim.
Shadows dance, with hidden grace,
In this realm, time slows its pace.

Voices carried on the breeze,
Whispers weaving 'neath the trees.
Ancient stories seek to find,
Those who listen, those who mind.

Moonlight drapes, a silver shroud,
Nature's chorus, soft and loud.
Every sigh, a tale untold,
In this magic, brave and bold.

So wander here, let heart be still,
Embrace the dark, obey the thrill.
In shrouded whispers, truth will gleam,
In the shadows, find your dream.

## **Silence of the Night**

The stars whisper soft tales,
Moonlight dances on the trees.
Shadows stretch across the fields,
In the hush, a gentle breeze.

Dreams drift like the fluttering leaves,
Wrapped in a silver embrace.
Quiet wonders fill the air,
In this tranquil, sacred space.

Crickets sing a lullaby,
The world rests, as time stands still.
In the silence, hearts find peace,
Night's sweet magic, a warm thrill.

The night holds secrets untold,
Veiled in the misty, dark hue.
In her arms, the world is calm,
Beneath the sky, a deep blue.

As dawn breaks, the night must go,
But memories linger on bright.
In the silence of the night,
We find solace, pure delight.

## Lurking in the Gloom

Shadows crawl on ancient walls,
Whispers echo through the night.
Faintest glimmers, truths concealed,
In the depths, there hides a fright.

Figures dance in corners dim,
Secrets murmur in the dark.
Every heartbeat quickens dread,
As mysteries begin to spark.

Footfalls soft, the air is thick,
A chill runs down the spine's track.
In the gloom, a presence stirs,
Whispers beckon, will you look back?

Time stands still in haunted sighs,
Figures fade with morning's light.
But in dreams, they linger still,
Lost in shadows, out of sight.

A tale woven in the night,
Of souls that wander, never home.
In the gloaming, fears take flight,
Where no light dares to roam.

## Embrace of the Dusky Sky

Sunset spills its colors wide,
Brush strokes blend in fiery sparks.
Clouds weave tales of whispered dreams,
As daylight softly, slowly darks.

The horizon kisses twilight,
Stars prepare to make their show.
In the dusky, tender light,
A serenade of night birds flow.

In this moment, worlds collide,
Day meets night in sweet embrace.
Nature pauses, breath held tight,
In the beauty of this place.

The sky, a canvas vast and grand,
Holds the secrets of our hearts.
In the dusk, a quiet promise,
As one day ends, another starts.

Wrapped in shades of purple haze,
We find solace, silence near.
In the embrace of the dusky sky,
Whispers of love, crystal clear.

## **Secrets in the Dimlight**

In corners where the shadows creep,
   Lies a world of stories told.
Beneath the dim, a heart will leap,
   In the twilight's gentle fold.

Flickering candles cast their glow,
   Illuminating paths unseen.
In the hush, the secrets flow,
Like rivers deep, serene, and keen.

Every flicker hides a tale,
Every whisper carries dreams.
In the dim, truth may prevail,
Unraveling what silence seams.

With each breath, a mystery wakes,
In the folds of the night's embrace.
Seeking light where darkness rakes,
   Finding warmth in a hidden place.

When dawn breaks, the secrets fade,
   But echoes linger in the soul.
   In the dimlight, unafraid,
We discover what makes us whole.

# **Faint Echoes in the Mist**

Whispers dance on morning dew,
Softly veiling what we knew.
Footsteps lost among the trees,
Carried gently by the breeze.

Shadows stretch and weave their tale,
Drawing us to where we pale.
Voices linger, faint and light,
Fading slowly into night.

Each breath caught in twilight's glow,
Silent secrets ebb and flow.
Memories woven, thin and frail,
Calling out, yet far more stale.

Misty veils that softly part,
Revealing echoes of the heart.
In the silence, truths unfold,
Stories long since left untold.

Yet we wander, never found,
In the echoes, lost, unbound.
Chasing dreams that drift and twist,
Faintly fading in the mist.

## Lament of the Concealed

Behind the curtain, shadows play,
Veiling dreams that drift away.
Voices linger in the dark,
Flickering light, a distant spark.

Hushed confessions fill the air,
Secrets whispered, filled with care.
Hidden hopes within the sighs,
Truths concealed from prying eyes.

Each heartbeat echoes in the night,
Fearing dawn's revealing light.
Yet within the quiet grief,
Lives the search for sweet relief.

In the silence, we reside,
Longing for what we must hide.
Still we yearn and still we ache,
For the bonds our hearts can break.

Hold the shadows close and tight,
Lamenting in the moon's pale light.
Yearning for the strength to heal,
In the sorrow, hearts concealing.

## **Threads of Obscurity**

Winding paths where shadows cling,
Threads of fate, we softly sing.
In the shadows, stories weave,
Tales of sorrow, love, and leave.

Colors blend into the night,
Lost in shades that dim the light.
Every whisper holds a chance,
To reveal the hidden dance.

Silent knots of time entwined,
Fragmented dreams we seek to find.
In the fabric, doubt and fear,
Every stitch holds echoes near.

Through the labyrinth we roam,
Searching for the threads of home.
Bound by shadows, lost in seams,
Waking slowly from our dreams.

Yet in darkness, sparks we see,
Glimmers of our history.
Threads of life, though tangled tight,
Guide us softly through the night.

## Navigating the Sable Sea

Sailing through the starlit gloom,
Bathed in night's embracing womb.
Waves of shadows, whispers deep,
Guarding secrets we must keep.

The compass spins, lost in thought,
Guiding dreams that time forgot.
In the void, our spirits float,
Carried softly, like a boat.

Every star, a distant voice,
Navigating, we have no choice.
Drifting where the shadows lie,
Hoping for a guiding eye.

Yet the sea is vast and cold,
Stories of the brave retold.
With each swell, our hearts beat bold,
Facing fears, life's truths unfold.

Through the sable depths, we sail,
With our hopes, we will prevail.
Navigating through the night,
Finding peace within the fright.

## Light Upon the Forgotten

In shadows deep where whispers lie,
A flicker stirs the darkened sigh.
The ghosts of time with dreams unmet,
Awake to find the sun has set.

Lost tales unfold in muted glow,
As ancient spirits start to flow.
They dance with joy, they dance with pain,
Reviving hearts once lost in rain.

Among the ruins, light will shine,
A beacon strong, a sign divine.
For every tear and every scar,
A history rekindles far.

So let us hear the silent pleas,
The echoes swaying in the trees.
For in the dark, we find the spark,
That guides us home from realms so stark.

## Embrace the Eclipsed

In twilight's grasp, the shadows play,
An astral charade, a hidden sway.
The moon wraps tight, the sun concealed,
A cosmic dance, our fate revealed.

Cast aside the doubts that cling,
And let the night begin to sing.
For in embrace, we find our truth,
A melding of the old and youth.

Each breath a whisper, soft and bold,
As stories of the night unfold.
The starlit skies forge bonds anew,
Reminding hearts of what is true.

With every pulse, the shadows swell,
A secret world where dreams do dwell.
So hold the night, let go of fear,
In eclipse's warmth, we draw near.

## The Lurking Symphony

In silence thick, the notes appear,
A symphony of joy and fear.
They lurk within the hidden bends,
Awakening where darkness tends.

Strings of fate pull gently tight,
As melodies take flight at night.
A haunting echo, soft yet grand,
Unfolds like grains of ancient sand.

Each chord a tale the shadows weave,
Of love and loss, of dreams we leave.
In every heartbeat, music flows,
A tapestry of highs and lows.

So listen close, let spirits guide,
Through veils of time, where hopes abide.
In lurid tones and vibrant dreams,
Awake the soul with whispered schemes.

## **Veiled Moments**

Beneath the light of fading day,
Veiled moments drift and softly sway.
They cloak the truth with silken thread,
Whispers linger where dreams are bred.

Behind the veil, the heart beats slow,
In hidden paths, we come to know.
The secrets lost in twilight's hue,
Reveal themselves in shades of blue.

Each fleeting glance, a world unseen,
In shadows where the stars convene.
A pulse of life, both soft and frail,
Encased in time's ethereal veil.

Let us embrace what's wrapped in hush,
In veiled moments, feel the rush.
For every breath that's caught in time,
Is but a note in life's sweet rhyme.

## **Echoes of Dusk**

The sun dips low, a fading glow,
Shadows stretch, begin to flow.
Whispers dance on whispered breeze,
Night unfolds with quiet ease.

Stars awaken, one by one,
As nightingale sings her song undone.
Echoes linger in the air,
Softly wrapped in twilight's care.

As lanterns flicker, dreams ignite,
Awakening the stars so bright.
Footsteps follow, soft and slow,
In the dusk where secrets sow.

The world, a canvas, bittersweet,
Each heartbeat marks a soft retreat.
In this realm, where shadows play,
Echoes linger, love's ballet.

With every whisper, hopes revive,
In the mute where dreams survive.
Beneath the veil of night, we see,
The echoes of what used to be.

## **Whispers Beneath the Veil**

In the quiet, secrets dwell,
Beneath the veil, where shadows swell.
Whispers float on gentle sighs,
Hushed confessions from the skies.

Moonlight drapes the world in grace,
Lost in time, we find our place.
Soft and sweet, the stories flow,
Ancient truths the night bestows.

Through the trees, a sigh escapes,
Nature holds our heart, it shapes.
In the dark, where futures gleam,
Whispers dance like a summer dream.

Stars wink down, kindred souls,
Linking hearts, parts of whole.
A moment captured, signed and sealed,\nIn the silence, truths revealed.

Beneath the veil, lies the creed,
That love and hope plant the seed.
Embrace the night, let it unveil,
The whispered dreams we must not fail.

## Secrets of Twilight

Twilight casts its gentle hue,
Secrets linger, born anew.
Softly spoken, shadows blend,
In twilight's arms, we transcend.

Golden hour, the world aglow,
Hints of mystery, ebb and flow.
As day surrenders to the night,
Whispers beckon, hearts ignite.

Horizon blurs with hues so soft,
Dreams take flight, like feathers aloft.
Promises made in fleeting light,
In twilight's grasp, all feels right.

Moments melt, like waxen tears,
Boundless hopes dispel our fears.
In this space where silence sighs,
Secrets linger beneath the skies.

With every heartbeat, joys resound,
In twilight's glow, our souls are bound.
We chase the dusk, beneath the spell,
Embracing secrets twilight tells.

## Beyond the Gloom

In shadows deep, we find our way,
Beyond the gloom of fading day.
Hope ignites like a distant star,
Guiding us, no matter how far.

Through the fog, where fears reside,
We summon strength we cannot hide.
Each step forward, a battle won,
In the dusk light, we find the sun.

Voices echo through the mist,
Promises made we can't resist.
With every heartbeat, courage grows,
Beyond the gloom, our spirit flows.

In darkened woods, where whispers loom,
We seek the light, dispel the gloom.
For in our hearts, a spark remains,
A beacon bright, when hope regains.

Together we rise, hand in hand,
Beyond the gloom, we'll make our stand.
With dreams alight, we will withstand,
The shadows fade at love's command.

## Fading Footsteps

Softly pound the earth beneath,
As shadows stretch and softly breathe.
Echoes dance in silent night,
Fading footsteps, lost from sight.

Memories whisper with the breeze,
In twilight's glow, they seek to please.
Each step taken, now a trace,
Lost in time, we find our place.

The path we walked, now overgrown,
In heart's own song, we're never alone.
Fading footsteps, tales to tell,
In quiet corners, they still dwell.

Time drifts gently, pulls away,
Yet in our hearts, they choose to stay.
Softly fade, yet still remain,
A haunting echo, lost refrain.

## Twilight's Embrace

The sun dips low in grace divine,
Night's tender arms begin to twine.
Stars awaken, wink and play,
In twilight's embrace, they softly sway.

Whispers of dusk, a gentle hush,
Nature sighs in evening's blush.
Colors blend in silken streams,
As daylight fades, we chase our dreams.

Shadows stretch and softly dance,
Underneath the moon's romance.
Each heartbeat in the cooling air,
Draws us closer, binds our care.

In this moment, time stands still,
Echoes of love, a soothing thrill.
Twilight's embrace, both warm and bright,
Guides us home through the tranquil night.

## **The Undercurrent of Time**

Beneath the surface, secrets hide,
Waves of time, a restless tide.
Flowing softly, drawing deep,
In whispered tales, we lose our sleep.

Moments rise like tide pools swell,
Memories crafted, stories tell.
Incurrent pulls, we drift along,
Caught in echoes of a song.

Time slips by, a silent thief,
Where joys and sorrows find belief.
Beneath the stars, the currents play,
Guiding hearts along the way.

Each tick a wave, each tock a shore,
Unseen forces we can't ignore.
As night gives in to dawn's own chime,
We find our place in the march of time.

**Across the Dim Path**

In the quiet, a path unfolds,
Muffled steps and secrets told.
Beneath the boughs where shadows cling,
A world unseen, where spirits sing.

The air is thick with whispered lore,
Of travelers past, who walked before.
Through tangled roots and leaves that sigh,
We wander where the echoes lie.

Each step a journey, each breath a choice,
In silence we hear the forest's voice.
Guided by stars that softly gleam,
We drift along this silver dream.

Across the dim path, hearts align,
In twilight's glow, our souls entwine.
With every heartbeat, the darkness fades,
And light breaks through the whispered shades.

## The Inward Quest

In silence deep, I seek my soul,
Through whispered dreams, I make it whole.
Each thought a thread, a woven light,
In shadow's embrace, I find my sight.

Reflection mirrors the heart's desire,
With each step deeper, I walk through fire.
Fear dances close, yet courage stays,
In the quiet depths, my spirit plays.

Amidst the chaos, I steal away,
To listen soft where echoes sway.
A hidden path that winds and turns,
In stillness, the brightest passion burns.

The journey twists, as moments weave,
A tapestry where I believe.
To honor the whispers, I gently tread,
An inward quest to what is said.

Through every falter, each stumble made,
The heart's soft song will never fade.
Each layer peeled, a truth unfolds,
In quest of self, the life retold.

## Surrender to the Haze

Wrapped in fog, the world feels light,
A gentle surrender, a dance in night.
Lost in the whispers of soft refrain,
A hidden joy beneath the pain.

Waves of uncertainty wash the shore,
While dreams drift softly, begging for more.
In this haze, let go of the fight,
Follow the shadows into the light.

The pulse of the heart, a silent call,
A breath of freedom in the fall.
In the fog, I'm found and free,
Surrendering sweetly to what will be.

Mysteries linger, shrouded in grey,
In the warmth of the haze, I choose to stay.
Each step a promise, each breath a chance,
To be embraced in life's gentle dance.

So let the mist wrap around my heart,
For in surrender, I find my art.
Floating softly, with trust I'll gaze,
Lost in the wonder of the haze.

## **Stories Untold**

Beneath the stars, a secret lives,
Whispers of time, the universe gives.
Each heartbeat echoes, a tale to share,
In shadows long, dreams linger there.

Paths of the past weave into the now,
With every choice, I take a bow.
Memories curl like smoke in the air,
To unveil the stories, raw and rare.

In the silence felt, the truths unfold,
Hidden chapters, both brave and bold.
Each story holds a lifeline true,
In the tapestry of me and you.

Let the words dance upon the page,
To capture the wisdom of every age.
In the stillness, where fears reside,
The stories untold, my heart will guide.

So gather round, let the tales arise,
Under the cover of starlit skies.
For every life, a story to mold,
In sacred space, the truths unfold.

## **Flickers of the Subtle**

In the gentle sway of the evening breeze,
Flickers of light dance with such ease.
A moment captured, a tear, a smile,
Subtle reminders to pause for a while.

Whispers of dusk paint the skies,
Colors blending where silence lies.
In the hush between breaths and sighs,
The universe speaks, where wonder flies.

Little things twinkle, the heart ignites,
Finding beauty in softest sights.
In the shadow of moonlight's embrace,
Flickers of dreams find their place.

With every heartbeat, a truth unfolds,
Soft like the stories that time holds.
In quiet corners, life slips through,
Flickers of subtle, I find what's true.

So heed the whispers, the delicate calls,
In the softest light, my spirit enthralls.
For in moments fleeting, I learn to trust,
Flickers of subtle, in this I must.

## Echoes of an Unwritten Tale

In the silence, words reside,
A story whispers, soft and wide.
Characters dance in fleeting light,
Pages waiting to ignite.

Unraveled dreams on paper's edge,
Each heartbeat forms a new pledge.
Forgotten tales, lost in the mist,
In the echoes, we persist.

Wandering paths of what could be,
Voices call from memory's sea.
Imagination's gentle sway,
Guides the tales yet sung today.

Ink drips slow, a measured flow,
Chasing shadows, to and fro.
A pen awaits its destined flight,
To craft the darkness into light.

Within the mind, a spark ignites,
As dormant tales take to new heights.
An unwritten world, vast and free,
Echoes linger, endlessly.

**Restless Reveries**

In twilight's grip, thoughts interlace,
Restless dreams in a silent space.
Wanderlust blooms in tender night,
Starry visions, taking flight.

Chasing whispers through the trees,
The heartbeats sway like summer breeze.
Sleep's embrace, a fleeting call,
Awake in dreams, we rise, we fall.

Echoes linger, memories blend,
In shimmering thoughts that twist and bend.
Faces blur in the dimming light,
Restless reveries take their flight.

A fragile dance upon the air,
Unraveled wishes everywhere.
Seeking solace in heart's refrain,
Capturing joy, defying pain.

The moon above, a guiding friend,
In sleepless nights that seem to end.
Restless spirits on journeys roam,
In dreams, we find our way back home.

## **The Murmuring Shadows**

In the twilight, shadows creep,
Secrets held that silence keep.
Softly whispered, tales untold,
In the dusk, the night grows bold.

Figures flit with ghostly grace,
Fleeting glimpses, a hidden face.
Curtains flutter, a breath of air,
Murmurs echo, everywhere.

A world reborn in evening's sigh,
Melodies run while the stars reply.
Dancing lights in a dusky glow,
The murmurs beckon, sweet and slow.

Hidden paths where dreams entwine,
Crimson streaks on the edge of time.
In shadows cast by fading light,
Stories stir, ready to ignite.

The night unfolds its velvet cloak,
In every breath, a whispered joke.
Murmuring shadows, truth they hold,
Secrets shared, yet still untold.

**Dreaming Under Dusk**

As day dissolves in hues of blue,
Night's embrace begins anew.
Stars awaken, softly glow,
Dreaming hearts begin to flow.

In twilight's grace, we find our way,
A canvas where our wishes play.
Each flicker tells a secret tale,
In twilight's arms, we shall not fail.

Whispers of the night draw near,
With every sigh, we shed our fear.
Drifting softly, our spirits glide,
Under dusk, our hopes abide.

A tapestry of light unfolds,
Filling hearts with dreams untold.
In this moment, we are free,
Dreaming under dusk's decree.

Time stands still as shadows merge,
Embracing thoughts, like tides they surge.
In dreams, we find our sacred trust,
Awake, asleep — it's all a must.

## **Unseen Horizons**

Beyond the mountains, dreams reside,
A whisper of hopes that swell and glide.
The sky paints stories in vibrant hues,
As twilight beckons with hidden clues.

Waves of the ocean softly embrace,
Carrying secrets to a distant place.
The winds carry tales of lands unknown,
Where all our wanderlust is brightly sown.

Stars emerge in the vast expanse,
Inviting the heart to a fleeting dance.
Each flicker a promise, shimmering bright,
Guiding our souls through the blanket of night.

In silence we walk, hand in hand,
Exploring the mysteries of this land.
With every step, new paths appear,
Unseen horizons whispering near.

Together we roam through the twilight's glow,
Chasing the dreams that ebb and grow.
In the soft embrace of the starlit dome,
We find in each other a final home.

## Shades of Solitude

In the corner of a quiet room,
Where shadows gather, dispelling gloom.
Time stands still, a gentle sigh,
In solitude's arms, we learn to fly.

A lone candle flickers in the dark,
Illuminating whispers that leave their mark.
Thoughts intertwine like vines on a wall,
In the stillness, there's beauty in it all.

Colors blend in muted grace,
As quiet moments fill the space.
The heart finds solace in whispered dreams,
In shades of solitude, life redeems.

Outside there's chaos, a distant pain,
But here, in silence, we're free again.
With every breath, we paint the air,
Finding ourselves in the depths of care.

Embrace the stillness where shadows play,
In solitude's arms, we'll find our way.
Each shade a story, rich and profound,
In this gentle haven, peace is found.

## The Silent Cascade

Water tumbles down the rocky face,
A silent cascade, nature's grace.
Whispers of wind through the leaves above,
Serenading the world with gentle love.

Rays of sunlight dance in the spray,
Creating rainbows in a delicate display.
Each drop a promise, a soothing sound,
In the heart of the forest, tranquility found.

Moss-covered stones wear a timeless cloak,
Amid the rush, there's magic spoke.
Life flourishes in the embrace of the stream,
In the silent cascade, we can dream.

Beneath the canopy, shadows play,
Where moments linger and time holds sway.
A symphony builds from a still retreat,
In nature's rhythm, we find our beat.

Leave behind worries, let your heart race,
Join the dance in this sacred space.
In the quiet waters, let life cascade,
Flowing softly, in peace we wade.

## In the Absence of Light

When shadows stretch in the fading day,
And echoes of laughter seem far away.
The heart feels heavy, wrapped in the night,
Craving the warmth of a flickering light.

Whispers of dreams fade into despair,
In the absence of light, we learn to bear.
Yet in the darkness, resilience shines,
With every heartbeat, a new hope aligns.

Stars twinkle softly, a distant glow,
Guiding lost souls who wander and slow.
In the quiet embrace of the cold, deep night,
We gather our courage, we rise to fight.

Moments of silence hold stories untold,
As hearts intertwine, weaving brave and bold.
In shadows, we find the strength to ignite,
A fire within that banishes fright.

So stand together, hand in hand, tight,
In the absence of light, we'll forge our own sight.
With love as our beacon, we'll navigate sorrow,
Creating our dawn, a bright new tomorrow.

## A Journey Beyond the Gloom

Beneath the heavy clouds we tread,
With shadows dancing at our feet.
Through winding paths, our hopes are spread,
In search of light, our hearts compete.

With every step, the darkness fades,
A flicker glows, a guiding star.
Through tangled woods and silent glades,
We find the strength to journey far.

The whispers call from distant streams,
As nature sings its ancient song.
In moonlit nights, we weave our dreams,
Together, where we all belong.

Each bridge we cross, a tale unfolds,
Of fears we faced and lessons learned.
In bonds of faith, our spirits hold,
The fire within, forever burned.

So onward, friends, through trials brave,
In unity, we'll rise anew.
A journey taken, souls to save,
Beyond the gloom, our skies turn blue.

## **Whispers of the Dark**

In shadows deep, the silence hums,
A secret world where whispers lie.
The night unveils its quiet drums,
As stars ignite the velvet sky.

Echoes of dreams in twilight mist,
A haunting call from long ago.
In every sigh, a tale persists,
Of lost loves and of long-felt woe.

The moonlight dances on the trees,
As shadows form a fleeting glance.
Here in the dark, we're free to freeze,
Our hearts entwined in midnight's trance.

With every breeze, a glimpse of hope,
As darkness weaves its tapestry.
In whispered vows, we learn to cope,
With fears that linger, silently.

In whispers soft, the dark confides,
The secrets held in sacred trust.
Through starry nights, we learn to bide,
To find the light, as all things must.

## Echoes in the Twilight

As daylight fades to dusky hues,
The tranquil skies begin to sigh.
In twilight's grasp, we find our muse,
Through whispered words, the moments fly.

A serenade of distant calls,
The world transitions, slowly sways.
In fading light, the memory sprawls,
Of laughter shared on summer days.

Beneath the arch of shadows cast,
We stand as one, our spirits bold.
In every echo from the past,
Are stories waiting to be told.

With every breath, a promise made,
That twilight holds a magic rare.
In gentle light, all fears displayed,
We step into the heart laid bare.

As stars emerge and dreams take flight,
We find our path where shadows blend.
In echoes soft of fading light,
A journey starts, our hearts extend.

## Beneath the Veil

In twilight's warmth, the secrets sleep,
Beneath the veil of dreams so bright.
With whispers soft and silence deep,
We seek the truths that dance in light.

The fabric woven, threads of fate,
In every stitch, a story weaves.
Through hopes and fears, we navigate,
Finding solace in autumn leaves.

Beneath the veil, the world transforms,
As shadows mingle with the day.
In gentle grace, the spirit warms,
To guide us on the hidden way.

With every sigh, the night unfolds,
In dusky shades, our hearts align.
A tapestry of tales retold,
In hidden realms where stars entwine.

So let us tread on paths unknown,
With courage bright, we'll face the night.
Beneath the veil, we find our own,
In every shadow, there's a light.

## Veils of Obscurity

In shadows deep, where secrets lie,
The whispers of the night softly sigh.
A mystery wrapped in silver mist,
Elusive dreams that time has kissed.

Through tangled paths, the lost winds roam,
Seeking solace in a world unknown.
Glimmers of truth in twilight's glow,
A dance of thoughts that ebb and flow.

Behind the veil, the heart does tread,
In search of words left unsaid.
The silence speaks, a tender call,
In darkness, we can lose it all.

Yet hope persists in twilight's gaze,
As stars awaken from their haze.
A spark ignites in the silent tear,
For tomorrow brings what we hold dear.

In the stillness, we must find,
The hidden paths of heart and mind.
For in the veils, we learn to see,
The beauty of life's mystery.

## **Twilight's Quiet Lament**

As sun dips low, the sky turns grey,
Daylight fades, whispers of decay.
Softly, the shadows stretch and creep,
While nature bids the world to sleep.

A fragile hush upon the land,
Where dreams drift lightly, hand in hand.
With every sigh, a story told,
Of fleeting moments, brave and bold.

The purple clouds, they drift and sway,
Embracing dusk, in soft array.
Each breath of night, a tender scene,
In twilight's arms, we find serene.

Yet in this peace, a longing brews,
For time to halt, for night to choose.
To linger on in dreams so sweet,
And find the solace hearts repeat.

When dreams unite in dusky light,
We weave our hopes within the night.
For in this quiet, love's lament,
We learn that dusk is heaven-sent.

# Cloak of Midnight

Underneath the velvet sky,
Midnight wraps the world in sigh.
Stars like jewels, they softly gleam,
Crafting shadows of distant dreams.

A cloak of whispers cloaks the trees,
Pushing away the haunting breeze.
In the stillness, time stands still,
As night unfolds its quiet thrill.

With every heartbeat, shadows sway,
In a dance that guides the way.
The moon, a guardian, watches near,
Casting light, dissolving fear.

Through the cloak, each secret flows,
In midnight's grasp, the magic grows.
A tapestry of soft embrace,
Where every soul can find its place.

In the silence, we hear the song,
Of all that's right, of all that's wrong.
Cloaked in midnight's gentle grace,
We find our truth, we find our space.

## In the Depths of Dusk

In the depths where shadows play,
The sun bids farewell to the day.
Colors bleed in twilight's sigh,
As day and night begin to vie.

The whispers rise, the echoes call,
A hidden world, unveiled to all.
Each color hue a reference lost,
In twilight's hand, we bear the cost.

Memories drift on the twilight breeze,
Nestled in the swaying trees.
The stars awaken, shy and bright,
To blink their tales on the canvas of night.

In the depths, our hearts collide,
With dreams that linger, fears that hide.
Each fleeting moment we embrace,
As dusk bestows its dusky grace.

So let us dance in shadows cast,
And cherish moments that won't last.
For in the depths of dusk's embrace,
We find the light we long to trace.

## **The Mirage of Memories**


In dusty rooms where echoes lie,
Faded whispers of days gone by.
Photographs worn by the hands of time,
Chasing shadows that once felt sublime.

Broken dreams float on the air,
Fragments lost, yet still we care.
Glimmers of joy, pain intertwined,
In every corner, what we left behind.

A gentle breeze through an open door,
Sways the curtains of days before.
We reach for moments that slipped away,
Yearning for night to blend with the day.

Beneath the stars, we dare to speak,
Of laughter shared and hearts that seek.
In the silence, their laughter grows,
A song of life that gently flows.

Yet time moves on, relentless flow,
Leaving us with what we know.
Mirages shimmer in the heat,
Memories linger, bittersweet.

## Silhouettes of Haunting

In the shadows where secrets dwell,
Figures dance with tales to tell.
Whispers echo in the night,
Silhouettes bathed in pale moonlight.

Fleeting glimpses of those we lost,
Haunting dreams, a heavy cost.
Their laughter lingers, soft and clear,
In every tear, they reappear.

Forgotten voices call my name,
In the dark, I play their game.
Memories merge with the chill of dread,
Silhouettes of all who have fled.

Restless spirits in the fog,
Clutching hearts like a moving bog.
Through the mist, I chase their light,
In the stillness, I find my fright.

Yet through the fear, I learn to see,
Each silhouette's a part of me.
In their dance, I find my place,
Embracing loss, a soft embrace.

# Chasing After the Veil

Through the mists where shadows creep,
I wander lost, in silence deep.
Chasing whispers on the breeze,
Veils of secrets, hearts that tease.

With each step, the fog unfolds,
Stories hidden, yet untold.
In the twilight, lost souls play,
Chasing echoes of the day.

Fingers brush the fading light,
Hoping to grasp what feels so right.
In the distance, I hear a song,
Calling me where I belong.

Yet darkness lingers, truth obscured,
Hearts betrayed, and love uncertain.
As I chase what lies ahead,
Will I find the words unsaid?

In this journey, I seek to unveil,
The hidden truths behind the veil.
Each whisper heard, a heart's reveal,
Through the shadows, I learn to heal.

## Delving into Darkness

In the depths where silence lies,
Darkness curls with unseen eyes.
Whispers beckon from the night,
Casting fears in pale moonlight.

Lost in thoughts that drift and sway,
Shadows linger, dreams betray.
Yet I venture deeper still,
Seeking echoes of my will.

Through the dark, I hear the call,
A haunting melody, rise and fall.
In the depths, I find my truth,
Through the pain, the edge of youth.

With every heartbeat, I embrace,
The quietude, the cold space.
In this void where fears collide,
I learn to dance, let go, and bide.

Emerging from the shades of gray,
I see light in a brand new way.
Delving deep, I found my spark,
A flame ignites within the dark.

## Lingering Afterglow

The sun dips low, a golden hue,
Whispers of light dance in the dew.
Shadows stretch, a gentle embrace,
Time suspended in this sacred space.

Memories linger, softly they fade,
In the twilight, dreams are made.
Hearts ignite with warmth and grace,
A fleeting touch, a sweet trace.

The night unfolds, stars align,
In the quiet, souls entwine.
Holding close the fading light,
A promise kept in the night.

As darkness falls, we still remain,
In the glow, we feel no pain.
A gentle sigh, the world in slow,
Everlasting, the afterglow.

## Echoes of Forgotten Times

In the attic, dust and dreams,
Silent echoes burst at the seams.
Photographs of laughter shared,
Whispers vanish, yet we cared.

Time stood still, yet swiftly rolled,
Stories whispered, yet untold.
Footsteps fade, but love remains,
Imprints left by joy and pains.

Old vinyl spins a haunting tune,
Moonlight spills through the evening's swoon.
With every note, memories revive,
In faded colors, we survive.

The past a treasure, so divine,
In every corner, hearts entwine.
Like moths to flame, we search the signs,
Finding hope in forgotten lines.

## **Beneath the Surface Glimmer**

Still waters hide the depths untold,
Beneath the calm, a world unfolds.
Mysteries linger, shadows play,
In silence, secrets drift away.

Ripples dance upon the skin,
Echoes call from deep within.
A shimmering light, faint yet bright,
Guiding the lost toward the light.

The heart beats slow, in rhythm found,
Beneath the surface, life abounds.
A hidden beauty in the night,
Glimmers softly, out of sight.

With open hearts, we dive so deep,
Into the waters, dreams we keep.
In every wave, the stories weave,
A tapestry of love to believe.

# Glistening in the Gloom

Amidst the shadows, hope appears,
A tender light through all our fears.
The night is thick, the air is cold,
Yet glimmers shine, brave and bold.

Stars are scattered, like scattered dreams,
Whispers ride on silent streams.
Each glint a promise, a gentle glow,
Guiding hearts where we must go.

Darkness drapes, a velvet shroud,
Still we shine, singing loud.
In the gloom, we find our way,
Sparkling bright despite the grey.

With every glance back at the night,
Glistening moments, pure delight.
In shadows deep, we rise and fall,
Yet even in darkness, we stand tall.

# **The Enigma Awaits**

In the forest deep, whispers flow,
Secrets of the night, soft and slow.
Mysteries wrapped in a velvet guise,
Awaiting the brave, who dare to rise.

Silent echoes dance on the breeze,
Carrying tales that aim to please.
Each shadow weaves a story anew,
In a tapestry of the unseen view.

Look beyond where the eye can see,
Unlock the gates of what might be.
For every path leads to a door,
The enigma waits, forevermore.

In the heart of night, truth does gleam,
Cloaked in the mist like a fleeting dream.
Embrace the unknown, take a chance,
For in darkness lies a curious dance.

So step through the veils of time and space,
Let your spirit soar and embrace.
The enigma beckons, hear its call,
In the silence of shadows, you may find it all.

**Where Light Meets Dusk**

At the edge of day, colors collide,
Gold and purple in a gentle slide.
Whispers of twilight grace the land,
Where dreams and reality gently stand.

The sun dips low, the horizon glows,
As night unfolds, the magic flows.
Stars awaken in the velvet sky,
Painting wishes like a lullaby.

Time holds its breath, a tranquil pause,
As nature gathers its evening applause.
Creatures stir in the fading light,
Preparing for the embrace of night.

In this meeting of worlds, hearts ignite,
Hope flickers and dances, pure delight.
In the hush of dusk, creation sings,
Where light meets darkness, joy brings wings.

So linger here as the shadows grow,
Feel the wonder, let your spirit flow.
In this sacred hour, let love bloom,
Where light meets dusk, dispelling gloom.

**Beneath the Silent Moon**

In a quiet glade, soft and wide,
The silver moon takes gentle pride.
Casting shadows on a crystal stream,
Whispering secrets, a mystic dream.

Underneath this celestial glow,
Hearts entwine, in tender flow.
Nature's lullaby, serene and true,
Beneath the silent moon, love grew.

Branches sway in a soft embrace,
While fireflies dance, a nightly grace.
Memories linger in the night air,
Carried softly without a care.

Here, time flows like the rippling tide,
As souls connect, no need to hide.
In shadows cast by this radiant sphere,
We find our peace, our whispers clear.

So let your heart be light and free,
Find solace in this harmony.
Beneath the moon's watchful face,
Love's gentle power, a warm embrace.

## Shadows Speak

In the quiet dim where shadows blend,
Voices of the past start to ascend.
Each silhouette holds a tale to share,
Secrets that linger in the cool night air.

With every flicker, memories stay,
Dancing softly, they find their way.
Between the light and the encroaching dark,
Shadows whisper, ignite the spark.

Silent stories of love and strife,
Lurking gently, the echoes of life.
They weave through the air, a haunting tune,
As darkness deepens beneath the moon.

Listen closely, let your heart align,
For the shadows hold what is truly divine.
In their embrace, wisdom lies deep,
In the morrow's light, it's ours to keep.

So walk in wonder when night takes flight,
Discover the magic that thrives in the night.
For shadows speak in a language rare,
Revealing truths when you stop and stare.

# Curfew of the Cosmos

The stars align in silent prayer,
A vast expanse, a midnight flare.
Galaxies hum their ancient song,
While time drifts gently, holding strong.

Nebulas weave in colors bright,
In cosmic dreams, we find the light.
With every pulse, the heavens speak,
In whispered tones, it's peace we seek.

Comets race through velvet skies,
Tracing paths where stardust lies.
Each twinkle holds a secret's spark,
As we wander through the dark.

A tranquil hush envelopes wide,
The universe, our faithful guide.
In the stillness, hearts unite,
Beneath the tapestry of night.

As dawn arrives, the curtain falls,
The cosmos answers silent calls.
In morning's grace, we find our place,
In the endless void, a warm embrace.

## Cacophony of Shadows

In the corners where darkness creeps,
Whispers rise from ancient deeps.
Voices clash in the midnight air,
Echoes mingling with silent despair.

Figures dance, elusive and sly,
Caught in the web of a fleeting sigh.
A cacophony of fears entwined,
In the heart of night, chaos defined.

Shapes blend and twist, a blurred parade,
Lost in the masquerade we've made.
Every flicker, a tale untold,
Where shadows linger, brave and bold.

The moonlight cuts through the thick haze,
Illuminating the shadowy maze.
In this interplay of light and gloom,
Accelerating the heart's quiet thrum.

Embrace the dark, it holds a key,
To parts of us we seldom see.
In shadows deep, we find our way,
A dance of souls till break of day.

## **Whispers of the Uncharted**

Beyond the maps, through mystic lands,
Where wild dreams slip through our hands.
Uncharted realms call out our name,
With promises of glory and fame.

Amidst the fog, a path unclear,
The heart beats loud, though filled with fear.
Each step a choice, each turn a chance,
To find the magic in the dance.

The horizon sings a siren's tune,
Beneath the watchful silver moon.
The stars align to guide our quest,
In search of treasures, we are blessed.

What secrets lie in the verdant glade?
What whispers echo in the shade?
In the uncharted, our spirits soar,
Through endless skies, we crave for more.

So let us wander, hand in hand,
Through poetry of this wild land.
In every moment, we'll leave a trace,
Of whispers lost in time and space.

**Forks in the Dark**

In shadows deep, the choices wait,
Paths diverge, sealed fate or fate.
Each fork a whisper, soft yet clear,
Guiding the heart through dreams and fear.

Turn to the left or venture right,
Lost in the maze of endless night.
With every step, the compass sways,
Navigating through the tangled phrase.

Moments linger in eerie hush,
As doubts arise, we feel the rush.
The road ahead, a blur, unsure,
Yet in our hearts, a fire pure.

So take a breath, embrace the sway,
For in the dark, we'll find our way.
Forks in the night lead to the dawn,
In every ending, a new yawn.

With courage forged in the depths we tread,
We'll journey forth with strength widespread.
For every choice, a tale to spark,
A life reborn from forks in the dark.

**The Dance of Obscurity**

In shadows where silence sways,
Whispers twirl in lost ballet.
Flickering dreams in muted hues,
Hidden tales the night imbues.

Beneath masks worn in dusky light,
Figures glide, both ethereal and slight.
In the corners of the unseen,
They weave stories, soft and keen.

Ghosts of laughter, echoes faint,
Moving to a tune, a ghostly saint.
Steps that linger, fade away,
In the dance of night and day.

A ballet of the heart's desire,
Chasing flames, a sacred fire.
Lost in the rhythm, grasping air,
Embracing illusions, unaware.

With every twirl, the shadows blend,
A fleeting moment, to transcend.
In the dance, we find the key,
To our souls, wild and free.

# Across the Gloomy Expanse

A canvas wide, shrouded in gray,
Where spirits roam and echoes play.
Silent winds trace lines of lore,
Whispers of life on a distant shore.

Beneath the weight of heavy skies,
Sullen thoughts like birds that fly.
Across horizons, shadows stretch,
A longing heart, a promise etched.

The ground beneath, cold and bare,
Each footstep sings of despair.
Yet across the gloom, a light glints,
Hope flickers star-like, never hints.

Through tangled thoughts, pathways roam,
In the vastness, we still seek home.
With every breath, we chase the dawn,
In the twilight's embrace, we're reborn.

Across the stars, a tale of plight,
In the night's arms, we find our light.
For even in darkness, dreams can soar,
And life whispers softly, forevermore.

## **Forgotten Footsteps**

Along the path where shadows lay,
Footsteps linger, lost in grey.
Each imprint hides a story's thread,
Of wanderers and words unsaid.

In softened earth, the memories wane,
A journey marked by joy and pain.
Barely traced in dusk's caress,
A reminder of life's vastness.

Time drifts like leaves in a stream,
Where once was hope, now fades the dream.
In silence, the past holds its ground,
While echoes of laughter fade, unbound.

Yet in the stillness, a spark ignites,
Footsteps dance in secret nights.
As if the earth remembers well,
The stories we dared, the dreams we fell.

So tread with care on this sacred land,
For every footstep is a gentle hand.
To embrace the past and bring it near,
In the echoes of life, we persevere.

## In the Wake of Dusk

The sky blushes with evening's kiss,
A gentle hush, a fading bliss.
In the wake of dusk, dreams unfurl,
As stars awaken, they gently swirl.

Moments linger like whispers soft,
Glimmers of hope in shadows loft.
The horizon's edge, a dance of light,
Cradling the day, bidding goodnight.

While the moon climbs in silent grace,
Embracing night with a tender face.
In twilight's arms, we find our peace,
A respite, a chance for sweet release.

Colors fade, in a painter's stroke,
Brushing the world where dreams evoke.
In this stillness, the heart beats slow,
In the wake of dusk, we come to know.

As darkness weaves its tapestry fine,
With every star, a hope we design.
In the quiet embrace, we feel it too,
In the wake of dusk, our dreams renew.

## **Breaths of the Invisible**

In shadows deep, whispers glide,
Soft secrets held, where dreams reside.
The air hums low, a gentle tune,
Invisible hands beneath the moon.

Veils of silence, soft and vast,
Moments linger, memories cast.
With every breath, a story spun,
Lives intertwined, two become one.

Time flows like mist through quiet trees,
Carries our hopes on wandering breeze.
Through the unseen, we learn to feel,
The bonds of love, the heart's reveal.

In the quiet, we find our peace,
As the world slows, our doubts release.
Together we breathe, we drift, we soar,
In the invisible, we seek for more.

Every sigh, a promise made,
In the hushed night, fears start to fade.
We gather the stars, we hold them tight,
In breaths of the invisible, we find our light.

## The Darkening Weave

Threads of twilight start to blend,
Weaving shadows, the night transcends.
Colors fade in whispered sighs,
A tapestry of hidden lies.

Nightfall drapes its solemn cloak,
Every heartbeat softly spoke.
Secrets slumber in every fold,
In the dark, their tales unfold.

Whispers twine in a tangled maze,
Lost in echoes of bygone days.
With each step, the shadows creep,
In the weave, what dreams we keep.

The moon peeks through a shroud of gray,
Guiding lost souls on their stray.
In the dark, the beauty thrives,
As the darkness, too, survives.

From dusk till dawn, the weave will spin,
Holding stories, forgotten kin.
Embracing fears, the unknown calls,
In the darkening weave, the silence falls.

## **Starlit Silhouettes**

Underneath a vast expanse,
Figures dance in night's embrace.
Shadows twist in silvery light,
Carving stories in the night.

Each silhouette, a tale untold,
In starlit dreams, we are bold.
Whispers echo from the skies,
In the darkness, hope never dies.

With every star, a wish set free,
Cascading through eternity.
Guiding hearts through endless night,
In starlit silhouettes, we find our light.

Through cosmic paths, we wander wide,
Connected souls, eternally tied.
In the glow of celestial song,
In each heartbeat, we belong.

As dawn approaches, shadows fade,
Yet in our hearts, the memories stay.
For every night, new stars ignite,
Lighting dreams in starlit skies.

## Chasing the Fading Light

In twilight's glow, we chase the day,
As colors shift and fade away.
Every ray, a fleeting spark,
Illuminating paths in the dark.

Footsteps echo on the ground,
In this dance, we're lost, we're found.
With every breath, we yearn to hold,
The beauty of stories, yet untold.

Through the haze, the shadows cling,
In the dusk, we find our wings.
As light recedes, we push ahead,
In the fight, our fears we shed.

Memories flicker like fireflies,
In every heart, a light still flies.
Chasing dreams 'til the night is new,
In the journey, we become true.

Though the sun may sink from sight,
Hope persists, a guiding light.
In every moment, brave the night,
Chasing the fading, we find our flight.

# **In the Embrace of Nightfall**

The stars blink softly in the dark,
A quiet hush wraps the lark.
Moonbeams dance on silver streams,
In night's embrace, we weave our dreams.

Shadows stretch across the land,
Time slips like grains from hand.
Focused thoughts drift in flight,
All is calm, all feels right.

Whispers of the wind do play,
Telling secrets of the day.
With gentle touch, the night unfolds,
A canvas painted in pure gold.

Crickets chirp their soothing songs,
While the nightingale hums along.
Underneath this vast expanse,
Lost in dreams, we find our chance.

In slumber's arms we gently sway,
Caught between dusk and new day.
Held by night's sweet, tender pull,
In the embrace, our hearts are full.

## Hues of Uncertainty

Colors blend and swirl around,
In the silence, lost is found.
A canvas drenched in doubt and fear,
Yet in chaos, truth draws near.

Brushstrokes lingering in the air,
Each hue tells stories rare.
Shadows deepen, lines obscure,
In uncertainty, we find allure.

Moments fade, yet linger long,
In the silence, we belong.
Facets glimmer, sparks ignite,
Within us all, there's endless light.

Fleeting thoughts like clouds adrift,
In each moment, a precious gift.
Together, we paint the unknown,
In love and dreams, we've surely grown.

Each stroke a cry to see the truth,
To wear the colors of our youth.
In shades of doubt, we tap the soul,
Crafting a life that feels whole.

## The Hidden Whispers

In the garden, secrets bloom,
Soft whispers dispel the gloom.
Petals fall like gentle sighs,
In the twilight, silence lies.

Mysteries weave through the dusk,
In quiet corners, whispers husk.
Trees sway with ancient tales,
Their stories carried on the gales.

A rustling leaf reveals a path,
Where dreams and hopes are free to laugh.
In shaded glens, our hearts confide,
By nature's side, we dare to glide.

Moonlit glimmers kiss the ground,
Echoes of the night surround.
In every breath, a hidden muse,
In whispered tones, we gently choose.

What tales reside in starlit night's grace?
In hidden whispers, we find our space.
With every sigh, we embrace the night,
Guided forth by its gentle light.

## Gravity of the Night

The night descends like soft velvet,
Wrapping all in shadows, quiet yet.
A pull that beckons, sweet and low,
In stillness, vastness starts to grow.

Stars flicker like distant dreams,
Drawing minds to open themes.
In the dark, our thoughts unite,
Weightless, floating, pure delight.

Each heartbeat syncs with the moon's glow,
Life's rhythm in the night's soft flow.
Gravity holds us in its hold,
In night's embrace, our hearts are bold.

Whispers echo through the air,
In twilight's grasp, we linger there.
Boundless space seems to conspire,
Igniting souls with a secret fire.

Time stands still beneath the sky,
In every breath, we live and sigh.
The gravity of night's deep call,
In its warmth, we lose it all.

## Underneath a Canopy of Stars

Underneath the velvet skies,
Whispers of the night arise.
Dreams take flight on silver beams,
While the world sighs soft with dreams.

Each twinkling light a story told,
Of wishes cast, of hearts so bold.
A gentle breeze begins to play,
Guiding hopes that drift away.

The cosmos cradles every sigh,
As time slips by, oh, so shy.
We dance beneath the endless glow,
In a waltz that ebbs and flows.

Night unfolds its mystic veil,
In its embrace, we cannot fail.
United under stardust's grace,
We find our love in this vast space.

A blanket woven from the night,
Cocooned in dreams, we take our flight.
With every heartbeat, we will trust,
In the magic woven into dust.

## **Treading the Unlit Path**

Treading softly on the ground,
In shadows deep, no light is found.
Each step echoes through the haze,
   As thoughts drift into a maze.

The whispers of the night remain,
   Calling softly through the pain.
With courage found in distant stars,
We journey forth, despite the scars.

A flicker shines in hearts long dim,
   Guiding souls on a silent whim.
    In every rustle, every sigh,
   Lies a truth we cannot deny.

With each breath, the shadows lean,
   Creating paths yet to be seen.
  Dare we step into the unknown?
With every heartbeat, we have grown.

In the stillness, the fear will fade,
   As dreams awaken, unafraid.
   The unlit path leads us anew,
To find the light that burns within you.

## Veiled in Mystery

Veiled in whispers, soft and light,
Secrets hidden from our sight.
The dusk is rich with tales untold,
In its embrace, the night is bold.

Mysteries dance on a gentle breeze,
Beneath the gaze of ancient trees.
Echoes linger in the air,
Each a story, each a prayer.

In shadows deep, the truth will bloom,
As stars unveil their silent room.
The cosmos hums a lullaby,
Inviting dreams to flutter by.

A tapestry of night unfolds,
Woven with threads of silver and gold.
In this quiet, we will see,
The magic wrapped in mystery.

Let the enigma take its form,
As hearts embrace the midnight warm.
With wonder, we explore the deep,
In every secret, love we keep.

## Serpent's Kiss of Night

In shadows coils a silent sigh,
The serpent's kiss, the stars comply.
With grace it moves, a dance so sly,
Beneath the watchful, moonlit eye.

Whispers curl like smoke in air,
Spilling secrets, softly rare.
Through tangled dreams, we dare to tread,
While echoes of the night are fed.

Veiled in dark, the world seems free,
Enchanted by its mystery.
Each breath a spell, each glance a spark,
Guided by the compass of the dark.

In the silence, shadows play,
Transforming night into soft day.
With every heartbeat, wisdom glows,
In the serpent's kiss, the magic flows.

So let us wander, hand in hand,
Through whispered dreams and starlit land.
To find the light that dances bright,
In the serpent's kiss of night.

## **Dances in the Penumbra**

Shadows sway with whispered grace,
A quiet dance in twilight's space.
Branches bow and leaves will twirl,
As night begins its velvet swirl.

Echoes linger, soft and clear,
In this realm where dreams appear.
Stars above begin to gleam,
While lanterns flicker, softly beam.

Footsteps trace the ancient ground,
In the hush, a song is found.
Moonlight drapes a gentle shroud,
Embracing all beneath its crowd.

Time unravels, slow and deft,
In the penumbra, all is left.
Hearts entwined in night's embrace,
Lost together in this space.

The dance continues, never ends,
Where light and shadow weave as friends.
A timeless rhythm, soft and grand,
In the twilight, hand in hand.

# The Last Light Fades

Crimson skies bleed into night,
Dimming hues, retreating light.
A final blaze, then softest gray,
The sun slips slowly, fades away.

Whispers of the day remain,
Echoes of laughter, traces of pain.
As starlight beckons, one last sigh,
We watch the final moments fly.

Colors blend in dusky streams,
Glimmers of the fading beams.
Each heartbeat synchronizes with,
The quietude that the twilight gives.

Shadows deepen, softly creep,
While the world begins to sleep.
In the stillness, we find our place,
Beneath the dusk's tender embrace.

Hope lingers in the night's cool air,
As stars emerge beyond compare.
Though daylight's warmth may cease to be,
In darkness, dreams are set free.

## **Murmurs Beneath the Surface**

Ripples dance on a silver pond,
Whispers carried, soft and fond.
Underneath, secrets lie still,
Waiting patiently, sharing will.

Fish dart beneath the tranquil waves,
In shadows where the silence braves.
Nature speaks in muted tones,
As life unfolds in gentle moans.

A heartbeats echo, soft and low,
Where the currents twist and flow.
Bubbles rise and vanish quick,
In the depth, a clock ticks thick.

Gentle waves crash on the shore,
Murmurs rise, then fall once more.
The rhythm of the water's song,
Reminds us where we all belong.

In this dance of lost and found,
Every sound a love profound.
Beneath the surface, life thrives deep,
In secrets that the waters keep.

# When the Sun Retreats

When the sun retreats from view,
Night unfolds in shades of blue.
Stars emerge, a brilliant sight,
In the canvas of the night.

Gentle breezes start to sing,
As the moon begins to bring.
Silver beams on dewdrop grass,
Time to pause, let moments pass.

Wildflowers close their weary eyes,
Embraced by the darkened skies.
Crickets call and shadows play,
While the world drifts into gray.

Softly wrapped in night's embrace,
We lose ourselves in time and space.
Echos linger, dreams set free,
In the hush, just you and me.

When the sun retreats from day,
Hope remains, it's here to stay.
In the silence, hearts ignite,
Forever dancing with the night.

## The Abyssal Echo

In depths where silence dwells,
Whispers drift on shadowed swells.
A call from depths, a haunting tune,
As darkness cradles the weary moon.

Forgotten dreams in currents sweep,
Past sorrows lie in waters deep.
Echoes rise, like misty sighs,
In the void where lost hope lies.

Beneath the weight of ancient tides,
Where hidden truths in silence bide.
The abyss holds secrets tight,
In the heart of eternal night.

With every pulse, the shadows sway,
The echoes of the past replay.
Through swirling depths, they twist and weave,
Stories spoken, yet none believe.

In the abyss, embrace the fate,
As echoes linger, they resonate.
In darkness deep, the voice will ring,
A haunting song that shadows sing.

## Flickering Through the Gloom

Amidst the haze, a flicker glows,
Through veils of night, a soft light flows.
Suspended dreams in shadows play,
Guiding souls lost on their way.

A candle's dance, so brief, so rare,
Chasing away the burdened air.
Hope ignites in the darkest rooms,
Flickering softly through the glooms.

Each moment's spark, a fleeting shine,
A promise whispered, sweet and divine.
In the shadows, hearts draw near,
Flickers of joy amidst the fear.

Through winding paths, the light shall roam,
In every heart, it finds a home.
Flickering flames in unity bound,
Rising softly, with hope profound.

In gloom's embrace, we seek the flame,
With every flicker, we reclaim.
Together, let our spirits bloom,
Flickering brightly through the gloom.

## **Threads of the Night**

In twilight's grasp, the threads align,
Weaving stories, yours and mine.
Stars are spun in cosmic seam,
Each glimmer holds a whispered dream.

Through velvet skies, the fabric flows,
In shadows deep, the mystery grows.
Tales are stitched with silver light,
Binding hearts in the vast night.

Each thread a hope, each knot a fear,
Binding destinies we hold dear.
With every pulse of the night's embrace,
Threads of fate weave in their place.

Softly they shimmer, softly they sigh,
In the tapestry where wishes lie.
We dance along this woven path,
Embracing night's gentle wrath.

Weaving dreams as dawn's light fades,
In the night's hands, our joy cascades.
Through every thread, love takes flight,
Binding us close in the threads of night.

## Exhale of the Dusk

As the sun dips low, a soft exhale,
Whispers of evening begin to unveil.
Colors blend in a gentle sigh,
As day bids farewell to the tired sky.

The world slows down, time takes a breath,
In the hush of dusk, life finds its depth.
Shadows stretch, embracing the light,
In this tranquil dance of day and night.

With each gust of wind, a secret's shared,
In the fading glow, the heart is bared.
The stars awaken, one by one,
In the exhale of day, the night's begun.

Nature's calm, a soothing embrace,
In twilight's arms, we find our place.
A moment paused in the evening's fold,
Revealing stories yet untold.

Beneath the canvas, dreams ignite,
As night blankets all in its quiet flight.
An exhale soft, a promise cast,
In the dusk's embrace, we hold steadfast.

## Beneath the Mask

In shadow's grip, we hide our pain,
Smiles painted bright, yet hearts in vain.
The world sees joy, but no one knows,
The silent battles, where sorrow grows.

Behind the laughter, secrets creep,
In every jest, a truth runs deep.
Masked faces walk through crowded streets,
Yet solitude is what the heart greets.

With every glance, a story concealed,
The mask protects, but wounds are revealed.
Longing for solace, for someone to see,
The fragile soul that longs to be free.

We yearn for a bond, a touch, a sign,
Yet we're bound by thoughts unrefined.
Will we unveil what we suppress?
Or stay adorned in our loneliness?

Each thread unwound, peace may arrive,
To shed the mask, to learn, to thrive.
In openness, our hearts align,
Beneath the mask, true love can shine.

# Dancing in the Abyss

In darkness deep, shadows entwine,
Whispers echo, the void's design.
We sway with fears, in the silent night,
Lost souls dance, beneath the moonlight.

The abyss calls, an alluring fate,
Step by step, spiral, we wait.
With trembling hearts, we dive right in,
Chasing shadows, where chaos begins.

Twisting and twirling, in reckless grace,
The nothingness holds a dreamlike space.
Through gaping voids, our spirits roam,
In the heart of darkness, we find our home.

Yet what lies there, beyond the fear?
A glimmer of hope, a voice so clear.
Dancing freely in the vast unknown,
In this abyss, we are not alone.

For in every dip, there's truth to find,
Embracing shadows, we redefine.
So let us waltz, let spirits fly,
Dancing in the abyss, we touch the sky.

# Chasing Lurking Figures

Through tangled woods, figures drift,
Phantoms of dreams, an ethereal gift.
Each rustle whispers, a story unfolds,
In the heart of night, where courage holds.

With wide-eyed wonder, we chase the spree,
Echoes of laughter, calling to me.
The shadows flicker, in playful dance,
Tempting the brave with a fleeting glance.

Yet lurking too, the doubts arise,
Haunting reminders in disguise.
As we traverse, the path grows dim,
Shadows encroach, our hopes seem slim.

But amidst the fear, a spark ignites,
In the depths of darkness, we find the light.
To chase the figures, we break the chains,
In every heartbeat, true freedom reigns.

So let us venture through the unseen,
Embrace the wonders, and never lean.
For in the chase, we find our truth,
Chasing lurking figures, reclaiming youth.

## The Other Side of Dawn

When night surrenders to morning light,
A canvas painted, dark takes flight.
Each hue unfurls with whispers of grace,
On the other side, a new embrace.

The stars retreat, as shadows fade,
Hope emerges, unafraid.
In soft-fallen hues, the world awakes,
As dreams dissolve, reality breaks.

With every ray, a promise made,
To cherish moments that life displayed.
Though storms may gather, and darkness loom,
The other side of dawn brings bloom.

In gentle warmth, our fears dissolve,
And in this light, our hearts evolve.
For every dawn, a chance to start,
To mend the fractures within the heart.

Embrace the day, its wonders found,
Rebirth awakens on sacred ground.
In the glow of hope, let sorrows wane,
On the other side of dawn, we gain.

## **Cultivating the Quiet**

In stillness deep, the heart takes flight,
Beneath the stars, a whisper bright.
Leaves murmur soft, the world retreats,
In sacred calm, the soul completes.

A tranquil breath, the mind does clear,
Nature's song, the only cheer.
In gentle rhythm, life does flow,
Among the shadows, love does grow.

The twilight hums, the twilight sighs,
Awake in dreams, the spirit flies.
With every moment, peace is sown,
In quiet fields, we find our own.

With every heartbeat, silence calls,
In softened light, our spirit sprawls.
Embrace the hush, let worries fade,
In this retreat, true joy is made.

So sit awhile, the world to share,
In tender grace, beyond compare.
Let love embrace, let kindness dwell,
In the quiet heart, all is well.

## Emptiness of Twilight

In twilight's arms, the shadows play,
The sun bows low, then slips away.
Colors bleed into serene night,
Whispered secrets take their flight.

The world lies hushed, as dreams ignite,
A canvas painted with soft light.
The gentle pull of endless skies,
Holds echoes deep of whispered sighs.

With every star that twinkles clear,
A memory formed, a story near.
In the emptiness, the heart extends,
Where time suspends and logic bends.

Silhouettes dance in muted grace,
Each fleeting thought a warm embrace.
The twilight hush, a balm so sweet,
In calm surrender, we retreat.

So linger here, where night begins,
With open hearts, let hope seep in.
For in the dark, we find our way,
In the emptiness, we softly stay.

## Pulse of the Night

The moon beats strong, a beacon bright,
Guiding those lost in the night.
Waves of silence pulse like the tide,
In every shadow, secrets hide.

Stars flicker softly, their watchful glow,
In the still of night, we come to know.
Each heartbeat echoes in the dark,
Awakening dreams, igniting a spark.

Breath of the night, tender and deep,
Woven with rhythms, we long to keep.
Embrace the whispers, the calls from afar,
In the pulse of the night, we find who we are.

The world asleep, yet alive and bold,
Stories of old in the night unfold.
With every glance, a wish takes flight,
Capturing dreams in sheer delight.

So let the night cradle us near,
With its gentle touch, we lose all fear.
For here in the dark, we breathe anew,
In the pulse of the night, we are true.

## **Cradled in the Dark**

In velvet black, the stars do sleep,
The world is quiet, shadows creep.
Cradled safe in night's embrace,
In solitude, we find our place.

With every breath, the heart finds peace,
In darkness wrapped, all troubles cease.
The echoes fade, the tempo slows,
In silent dreams, our spirit grows.

Beneath the moon's soft silver hue,
Each fleeting thought, a trail of dew.
The universe cradles, arms spread wide,
In the depths of night, we gently hide.

Awake in whispers, the deep serene,
In shadows draped, our souls convene.
With open hearts, we softly glide,
Through the dark's embrace, we take our ride.

So rest awhile, let worries stray,
In the night's cradle, we find our way.
For in the dark, we're never alone,
In the gentle night, our truth is grown.

## The Forgotten Glimmer

In shadows deep, a light once burned,
Whispers echo, lessons learned.
Flickering hope in twilight's grace,
A gentle touch in time and space.

Memories linger, soft and bright,
Stars emerge from endless night.
Though paths may fade and dreams grow dim,
The heart's resolve will never swim.

Amidst the dark, a flicker stays,
Guiding souls through night's long maze.
With every tear, a seed is sown,
For in our hearts, light is grown.

Beneath the weight of doubt we stand,
Together still, hand in hand.
Through silence bold, we find our song,
In unity, we still belong.

The glimmer fades, yet hope remains,
Through endless loss, love's fire gains.
From shadows cast, we rise anew,
A forgotten glimmer shining through.

# Fragments of the Unknown

Each whispered thought, a fleeting trace,
A puzzle lost within time's embrace.
In shadows deep, we search in vain,
For pieces lost, yet still remain.

In every heart, a question beats,
Echoes linger on empty streets.
Through whispers soft, we seek to know,
What lies beyond the veils of woe.

Lost in dreams, we find our way,
Through shards of light and shades of gray.
Each fragment holds a tale untold,
Of love, of loss, of courage bold.

In scattered thoughts, a truth will flare,
For in the dark, we learn to care.
With every step, we piece the night,
The unknown fades, revealing light.

Though fear may loom, we dare to tread,
Through signs and symbols overhead.
In fragments found, our spirits soar,
Discovering worlds we've yet to explore.

## **Resilience in the Gloom**

When shadows creep and voices wane,
A silent strength defies the pain.
In darkest nights, we raise our heads,
With weary hearts and dreams unsaid.

Through stormy skies, we stand our ground,
In courage deep, our hearts are found.
For every tear that seeks to drown,
We build a bridge from lost to found.

In whispers soft, we'll find our way,
Resilience blooms with each new day.
Though gloom may linger, hope will spark,
To light our paths through endless dark.

Together still, we face the night,
With hands entwined, we hold on tight.
A family forged in trials' fire,
We rise to meet our heart's desire.

So let the world throw what it will,
Our spirits strong, our hearts will thrill.
In every shadow, we will bloom,
With love as light, we banish gloom.

## Mists of Yesterday

In fading whispers of the past,
Where memories like shadows cast.
The mists arise, a haunting song,
In twilight's glow, where we belong.

Each moment captured, slipping slow,
Through fingers grasping all we know.
Yet in the haze, we laugh and weep,
For moments lost, forever keep.

Through veils of time, we trace our steps,
In silent dreams, our hearts adept.
We dance with ghosts of what has been,
In every sigh, the truth begins.

The stories linger, rich with pain,
Yet joy emerges through the rain.
For in the mists, we find our grace,
A tapestry of time and space.

So let the past weave through our days,
Embrace the light within the haze.
In mists of yesterday, we see,
The heart's journey, wild and free.

## Flickers of the Unknown

In twilight's grasp, shadows dance,
Whispers call in a fleeting chance.
Ghostly lights flicker, fade away,
Mysteries linger at the end of day.

Through misty paths where secrets lie,
Echoes of laughter, a muted sigh.
Stars like fireflies softly blink,
Painting the night with thoughts to think.

Veils of silence conceal the truth,
Fragments of dreams from lost youth.
Each flicker guides with a gentle hand,
To realms uncharted, a distant land.

Paths unwoven, stories untold,
Chronicles hidden, waiting for bold.
Weaving the fabric of unseen fate,
A tapestry formed, yet never too late.

The heart beats softly, a rhythmic song,
In the unknown where we all belong.
Embrace the shadows, let them flow,
For in the flickers, our spirits grow.

# Heartbeats in the Abyss

In the depths where silence reigns,
Pulse of darkness, whispering pains.
A heartbeat thunders, wild and free,
Echoing tales of what's yet to be.

Drifting shadows, spirits entwined,
A dance of fate, so undefined.
Caught in a web of lost desires,
The abyss flickers with hidden fires.

Glimmers of hope in the endless night,
Guiding the lost with soft twilight.
Each beat a promise, each echo a call,
In the abyss, we may rise or fall.

Mists swirl thick with secrets deep,
Holding the dreams that we dare to keep.
In the wide chasm, fear intertwines,
Yet from the darkness, a light still shines.

To hear the heart's tune, a melodious hymn,
In shadows cast where the light grows dim.
For even in depths, our spirits can soar,
Through heartbeats in the abyss, we explore.

## Muffled Dreams

In silent chambers, echoes play,
Muffled whispers of dreams on display.
Softly they linger, fading away,
A tapestry woven in hues of gray.

Lost ambitions, shadows that creep,
Waltzing on edges of waking sleep.
Voices of wishers, hauntingly sweet,
Call from the depths, where longing meets.

Fleeting moments like clouds of mist,
In the corners of hearts, they twist.
Silent reminders of what might be,
Erased by the laughter of reality.

Fragments of wishes, drifting far,
Guided by the light of a distant star.
Each muffled dream, a delicate thread,
Stitching the patterns of words left unsaid.

Among the silence, hope finds a way,
In muffled dreams, we dare to stay.
For each whispered thought can ignite a flame,
Awakening desire to never be tame.

## Shades of the Unseen

In corners dark where shadows dwell,
Lie the secrets we seldom tell.
Shades of the unseen softly drift,
Carrying stories, a timeless gift.

In the silence, a whisper grows,
A vision veiled in twilight's prose.
Hues of longing paint the night,
In the depths of mystery, we find our light.

Each glance unshared, a silent plea,
Painting life's canvas for hearts to see.
In the shades we harbor our fears,
Yet weave them softly through laughter and tears.

Glimmers of truth in the fog unwind,
Drawing us closer, hearts intertwined.
Into the shadows, we cast our dreams,
For in the unseen, nothing's as it seems.

A dance of silence, a shroud of grace,
Embracing the unknown, we find our place.
In shades of the unseen, our spirits soar,
For what we cannot see opens the door.

## **Beneath the Watching Stars**

Under the blanket of shimmering night,
A tapestry woven, a celestial sight.
Whispers of dreams dance on the breeze,
In stillness, our hearts find sweet ease.

Glimmers of hope linger in the air,
Each spark a promise, a wish laid bare.
Moonlight caresses the slumbering earth,
As silence envelops, inviting rebirth.

We gaze at the wonders, infinitely wide,
Lost in the cosmos, where secrets reside.
Together we wander, hand in hand,
Among constellations, in stardust we stand.

The night holds our stories, tucked in its fold,
In patterns of beauty, both gentle and bold.
Beneath the stars, we find our place,
Eternal connections, a sacred grace.

So let the night carry our dreams afar,
As we share our hearts beneath the watching star.
In the firmament's glow, our spirits ignite,
Forever united, in love we take flight.

## When Darkness Speaks

In shadows where silence weaves its thread,
A quiet reminder of fears left unsaid.
Voices of anguish whisper and sigh,
When darkness speaks, we learn to defy.

The weight of the night can blur our sight,
Yet flickers of truth pierce through the fright.
Courage emerges from depths we despise,
Bathed in the lessons that darkness supplies.

In the heart of despair, a flicker of flame,
Each droplet of struggle, a whispering name.
Resilience blooms in the cracks of the soul,
When the night is heavy, we find our whole.

So listen closely to the tales of the dark,
For within its embrace lies the brightest spark.
The journey may twist through sorrow and grief,
Yet in the shadows, we find our belief.

When darkness speaks, let it echo within,
A symphony flowing, where hope can begin.
With every exhale, we shed what we lack,
Emerging from shadows, we venture back.

## Eclipsed Aspirations

Beneath the veil of an astral embrace,
Dreams linger softly, leaving a trace.
When shadows obscure what we hold dear,
Eclipsed aspirations rise through the fear.

The universe whispers in breaths of despair,
Yet hope's gentle pulse lingers in air.
Among the dimmed stars, a flicker resides,
A flickering candle that forever abides.

Faith dances lightly on the edge of a tear,
In moments of doubt, it draws ever near.
Through twilight's embrace, we courageously roam,
Finding our strength in the call of the unknown.

With each passing shadow, we learn to stand tall,
Embracing the darkness, it teaches us all.
For hidden within every transient pain,
Eclipsed aspirations are never in vain.

So let us awaken to dreams we ignite,
Guided by stars that shimmer at night.
Embracing each challenge with unwavering grace,
In the depths of our soul, we will find our place.

## The Adrift Light

In the ocean of thought, where memories play,
A flickering beacon lights up the way.
Waves crash with secrets, both tender and bright,
We chase after shadows, the adrift light.

Through turbulent waters, our hearts start to seek,
Glimpses of wisdom in moments unique.
Anchored in longing, we venture and roam,
Finding our solace, in tides that feel home.

The stars hold the stories of all that we yearn,
With each gentle flicker, our passions return.
In silence we ponder the paths left untread,
The whispers of journeys ignite what is said.

Time dances lightly, a sailor at play,
Charting the course through the night and the day.
Though winds may be fickle, and storms may arise,
We'll navigate boldly, guided by skies.

As light drifts away on the horizon's embrace,
We'll find strength in shadows, and courage in grace.
For though we may wander, our spirits unite,
Forever adrift, in the glow of the light.

## **Secrets Drifting in Silence**

Whispers float in the cool night air,
Echoes of dreams beyond compare.
Hidden truths in a silent embrace,
Lost in the shadows, a timeless space.

Winds carry tales of the unseen,
Veiled in darkness, a quiet sheen.
Each heartbeat sings a muted song,
In the stillness, where we belong.

Beneath the stars, the secrets glide,
With moonlit paths, our hearts confide.
Glimmers of hope in the quiet glow,
Drifting softly, as whispers flow.

Time suspends in these sacred dreams,
Laden with mystery, sweet as it seems.
Together we wander, where shadows sigh,
Secrets afloat in the vast night sky.

In silence, we learn the language of trust,
Unraveling stories, like stardust.
Every glance, a silent decree,
In this hush, just you and me.

## Shadows of the Heart

In the twilight, feelings collide,
Shadows of love we cannot hide.
Soft whispers brush against the night,
In the dark, the soul takes flight.

Echoes linger in the hesitant air,
Caught in the spaces, a tender snare.
Fleeting glances, an unspoken bond,
In the silence, our hearts respond.

Flickering hopes like flames in the void,
Something precious, never destroyed.
Beneath the surface, affection glows,
In the shadows, where the heart knows.

Paths intertwined, yet struggles remain,
Searching for solace through joy and pain.
In every heartbeat, shadows play,
Tales of the heart navigate the gray.

With each pulse, secrets intertwine,
In the shadows, our love will shine.
In the silence of night, we dare to be,
Trusting bravely, hearts wild and free.

# **Tides of the Unseen**

In the depths, the waters sway,
Tides of change pull us away.
Whispers hide 'neath crashing waves,
Secrets held, that the ocean saves.

Drifting currents reveal and conceal,
Fates are spun, hearts start to heal.
Moonlit dances on rippling streams,
Carrying our forgotten dreams.

In the ebb, we find what we seek,
Silent prayers on lips that speak.
Each draw of the tide tells a tale,
Of love's journey, of hope's trail.

Beneath the surface, mysteries dwell,
In whispered waves, the stories swell.
Laojit struggles with every crest,
In the waves, we find our rest.

Through the dusk, as daylight fades,
In the ebb of night, our hearts cascade.
Tides that rise and fall like dreams,
Unseen forces guide our seams.

**Cloaked in Mystery**

Wrapped in shadows, the night unfolds,
Stories whispered, yet untold.
In the silence, the unknown waits,
A tapestry woven with fragile threads.

Echoes linger in the dusky light,
Every gaze hides a secret delight.
In the corners where the shadows play,
Cloaked in mystery, we drift away.

Each heartbeat echoes with untold lore,
Moments captured, forevermore.
Beneath the stars, our paths entwine,
In the darkness, a love divine.

With every heartbeat, whispers grow,
A dance of secrets in the shadowed flow.
Veiled in dreams, our spirits rise,
In the stillness, where truth lies.

Together we walk through night's embrace,
Treading softly in our sacred space.
In this mystery, we find our way,
Cloaked in love, forever we stay.

## Mirage of the Forgotten


In the sands where whispers dwell,
Shadows dance, they weave a spell.
Fading echoes, stories old,
In the silence, dreams untold.

Moonlight casts a fleeting glow,
Memory's tides begin to flow.
Glimmers of a vanished past,
Fragile moments, shadows cast.

Footsteps lost, a wandering heart,
Through the mist, we drift apart.
Yet in twilight's soft embrace,
Time suspends, a sacred space.

Mirages form in veils of light,
Guiding souls through endless night.
Yet beneath the shifting sands,
Hope remains in distant lands.

In the void where dreams reside,
We chase the phantoms that abide.
Though forgotten, not erased,
In the heart, their warmth is chased.

## **Woven in the Twilight**

Beneath the sky of indigo,
Whispers weave, the shadows flow.
Golden threads of fading light,
Dance upon the edge of night.

Stars awaken, softly gleam,
Cradled dreams in twilight's seam.
Colors blend in silent grace,
Nature's art, a warm embrace.

Echoes of a twilight song,
Guiding hearts where they belong.
Mysteries in shadows cast,
Tales of futures, echoes past.

Time unwinds in soft refrain,
Moments fleeting, yet remain.
Woven tales in evening's glow,
As the gentle night winds blow.

In this realm of dusky peace,
Where the world finds sweet release.
Each heartbeat, rhythm divine,
In the twilight, spirits shine.

## **The Forgotten Horizon**

Beyond the peaks where shadows lie,
Forgotten dreams drift, caught in sighs.
Horizons lost to memory's hold,
Silent tales waiting to unfold.

Waves of time rise, then disperse,
In the stillness, we immerse.
Fleeting glimpses, visions fade,
Yet in their wake, a path is laid.

Mountains loom with ancient grace,
Guardians of a hidden place.
Whispers echo, distant and free,
Guiding wanderers by the sea.

In the twilight, shadows stretch,
Moments linger, heartstrings etch.
Though forgotten, they remain,
In the silence, seek the gain.

The horizon beckons, vast and wide,
Holding secrets deep inside.
With every step, the journey calls,
To uncover truth within its walls.

## Haunting Beauty

In the stillness, whispers rise,
Haunting beauty cloaked in sighs.
Moonlit paths and shadowed dreams,
Painting life in silver beams.

Each glance holds a soft goodbye,
Echoes caught in starlit sky.
Fragile hearts and silent tears,
Cherished moments turn to years.

Fleeting joy, a gentle trace,
Beauty dwells in time's embrace.
Like a ghost, it slips away,
Yet in memory, it stays.

A haunting song that softly plays,
Through the nights and endless days.
In the shadows, love shall bloom,
Whispers brightening every room.

For in the depths of every pain,
Lies a beauty that remains.
Haunting hearts, forever free,
In the silence, love's decree.

Milton Keynes UK
Ingram Content Group UK Ltd.
UKHW022224251124
451566UK00006B/110